Facts About the Mexican Wolf

By Lisa Strattin

© 2016 Lisa Strattin

Facts for Kids Picture Books by Lisa Strattin

Agouti, Vol 94

Red Footed Tortoise, Vol 95

Wood Stork, Vol 96

Wood Bison, Vol 97

Mexican Red Knee Tarantula, Vol 98

Rose Breasted Cockatoo, Vol 99

Pilot Whale, Vol 100

Skua, Vol 101

Lorikeets, Vol 102

Albino Squirrel, Vol 103

Sign Up for New Release Emails Here

http://lisastrattin.com/subscribe-here

Join the KidCrafts Monthly Program Here

http://KidCraftsByLisa.com

All rights reserved. No part of this book may be reproduced by any means whatsoever without the written permission from the author, except brief portions quoted for purpose of review.

All information in this book has been carefully researched and checked for factual accuracy. However, the author and publisher makes no warranty, express or implied, that the information contained herein is appropriate for every individual, situation or purpose and assume no responsibility for errors or omissions. The reader assumes the risk and full responsibility for all actions, and the author will not be held responsible for any loss or damage, whether consequential, incidental, special or otherwise, that may result from the information presented in this book.

I have relied on my own observations as well as many different sources for this book and I have done my best to check facts and give credit where it is due. In the event that any material is used without proper permission, please contact me so that the oversight can be corrected.

Table of Contents

INTRODUCTION 7

CHARACTERISTICS 11

APPEARANCE 13

LIFE STAGES 15

LIFE SPAN 19

SIZE 21

HABITAT 23

DIET 25

FRIENDS AND ENEMIES 27

SUITABILITY AS PETS 29

MEXICAN WOLF PUZZLE 39

KIDCRAFTS MONTHLY SUBSCRIPTION PROGRAM 40

INTRODUCTION

The Mexican wolf, commonly known as "El lobo," is gray in color with brown fur coating on its back. They have long legs with a sleek body enabling them to be fast runners. In the US, the Mexican wolf was in thousands for years, but was wiped out by mid-1970s in the wild. Only a handful then existed in zoos. In 1998, eleven Mexican wolves in a research program to restore their population were released back into the wild of Arizona to try to reestablish the wild population.

The numbers have grown slowly since then; but they still remain the most endangered subspecies of the wolf family in the world.

The Mexican wolf was the top dog in the borderlands and if their population returns, scientists believe they will restore the balance to the Southwest's ecosystem by keeping deer, elk and javelin numbers healthy and in check.

The Mexican wolf was believed to strengthen the animal population by preying on the old, sick and young, thereby preventing overpopulation and overgrazing of other animals.

CHARACTERISTICS

The Mexican wolf is the smallest of the North American grey wolves, with an average length of no more than 54 inches and a maximum height of 32 inches. The weight ranges from 60 to 100 pounds. They are listed as endangered mammals.

They have long legs with a sleek body built for running, with the grey appearance designed for superb camouflage in the forested areas of Arizona. They have a superior sense of smell that helps with hunting. They are known to move in packs like all wolves species for safety and higher chances of catching prey.

APPEARANCE

Apart from the characteristics already stated, the Mexican wolf has small but sensitive ears and small eyes with amazing eyesight. The wolves will move their ears from side to side in determining where the sound of prey is coming from. They can see and smell prey from a great distance.

The Mexican wolf's body is very powerful. This helps with killing the large and small prey that it hunts. The wolf has two fur layers, the top has long, coarse fur that keeps the wolf dry (guard hairs). The other coat is short, and this layer keeps the wolf warm.

Mexican wolf's toes spread apart preventing them from sinking deep into the snow. They have four toes on the hind feet and five on the front feet.

LIFE STAGES

Mexican wolves breed annually, mostly between January and March, and then it is only the pack leader (male and his female). Their gestation period is about 63 days, with an average of 4-6 pups born in April or May in a litter.

The pups are born both blind & deaf weighing about a pound. The first three weeks the pups are nursed 4 to 6 hours per day and the mother stays with them in the den to regulate their body temperature. The males during this time hunt and bring food back to the den, along with other members of the pack.

Pups are weaned at 8 weeks old. They can start to eat solid food regurgitated by the female and other members of the pack. It's during this time they are moved to "rendezvous sites" and spend the rest of the summer learning from the pack members how to live as a wolf.

After 6 to 8 months the pups are taken along with the pack and join in the hunts.

LIFE SPAN

The Mexican wolf in the wild can live for an average of four to five years, but they live for as long as 15 years in captivity. The short life span in the wild is attributed to them catching diseases, starvation and injuries.

Those living near humans have even a lower life span. Some of them are hit by cars accidentally.

SIZE

Mexican wolf size varies with the habitat locality. An adult wolf is about 54 inches long, from the tail to the tip of their nose. Their height is about 32 inches from shoulders to the toes and they generally weigh between 60 to 100 pounds.

Female are known to be a bit smaller than the males. The Mexican wolf is generally smaller than the northern species of wolves.

HABITAT

Mexican wolves are known to live in a wide variety of habitats, which ranges from prairies to forests, arctic tundra and pretty much anywhere there is availability of prey.

DIET

Mexican wolves mostly hunt large hoofed mammals like the mule deer, white-tailed deer and elk. They will also eat smaller animals such as rabbits, ground squirrels, jabelinas and mice.

When they are near humans, they have been known to hunt the livestock on ranches, leading to ranchers hunting them to stop them from killing their herds.

FRIENDS AND ENEMIES

The main enemy of Mexican wolf is humans, because of the illegal hunting of them for their skin. Unless in captivity they don't tolerate friends as they live in packs and will fight any competition.

SUITABILITY AS PETS

Mexican wolves are wild mammals and never belong in captivity as pets. Most people try to tame them into pets, but captive wolves still retain their natural hunting instincts from their parents.

People misinterpret the Mexican wolf unruly behaviors as normal dog aggression but it is not the same at all. Mexican wolves as pups behave just like dogs playful and relatively submissive, as they approach maturity they complete show themselves as predators, wide-ranging, pack oriented, and highly territorial.

Please leave me a review here:

http://lisastrattin.com/Review-Vol-112

For more Kindle Downloads Visit Lisa Strattin Author Page on Amazon Author Central

http://amazon.com/author/lisastrattin

To see upcoming titles, visit my website at LisaStrattin.com – all books available on kindle!

http://lisastrattin.com

MEXICAN WOLF PUZZLE

You can get one by copying and pasting this link into your browser:
http://lisastrattin.com/mexicanwolfpuzzle

KIDCRAFTS MONTHLY SUBSCRIPTION PROGRAM

Receive a Box of Crafts and a Lisa Strattin Full Color Paperback Book Each Month in Your Mailbox!

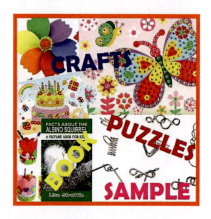

Get yours by copying and pasting this link into your browser

http://KidCraftsByLisa.com

Made in the USA
San Bernardino, CA
07 December 2016